The Hidden Wonders of Polish Wildlife

How to Explore and Protect the Biodiversity of Poland

MelLow Print

About The Author

MelLow Print is a passionate author who loves to create low content books relating to diverse countries, traditions, festivals etc. He believes that books are powerful tools to inspire, educate and entertain people of all ages and backgrounds. He enjoys exploring new places and cultures, and sharing his experiences and insights with his readers.

Table of contents

Introduction

Chapter 1
The Białowieża Forest: The Last Primeval
Forest in Europe
Location and size
History and importance
Threats and challenges
Conservation efforts
Flora and fauna

Chapter 2
The Tatra Mountains: The Roof of Poland
Location and size
History and importance
Zones and habitats
Flora and fauna

Chapter 3
The Baltic Coast: The Land of the Sea Eagles
Location and size
History and importance

Introduction

Poland is a fascinating country with a rich and diverse wildlife. From the majestic European bison in the ancient Białowieża Forest to the elusive lynx in the snowy Tatra Mountains, Poland offers a glimpse into the natural wonders of Europe. In this book, I will introduce you to the amazing wildlife of Poland and will also share with you some of the best places to observe and photograph them in the wild.

The purpose and scope of this book is to provide a comprehensive and accessible guide to the wildlife of Poland. I will cover the main animal groups that can be found in Poland, such as mammals, birds, reptiles, amphibians, fish, and insects. I will also describe the different regions and ecosystems of Poland, such as the Baltic Coast, the Central Lowlands, the Białowieża Forest, the Tatra Mountains, and the Carpathian Foothills. For each region, I will highlight the most characteristic and interesting species, their distribution, population, threats, and conservation efforts.

To give you some background information on Poland, here are some facts and figures that will help you understand its geography, climate, history, and culture, and how they affect its wildlife. Poland is located in Central Europe, and has a land area of about 312,696 square kilometers (120,733 square miles). It is bordered by Germany, the Czech Republic, Slovakia, Ukraine, Belarus, Lithuania, and Russia (Kaliningrad Oblast). It also has a coastline of about 440 kilometers (270 miles) along the Baltic Sea. Poland is divided into 16 administrative regions, called voivodeships, which are further subdivided into counties and municipalities. The capital and largest city of Poland is Warsaw, with a population of about 1.8 million people.

Poland has a temperate transitional climate, which means that it has four distinct seasons: spring, summer, autumn, and winter. The climate is influenced by the Atlantic Ocean, the continental air masses from the east, and the mountain ranges from the south. The average annual temperature is about 8.5 degrees Celsius (47.3 degrees Fahrenheit), but it varies widely depending on the region and the altitude. The warmest region is the southwest, where the average temperature is about 10 degrees Celsius (50 degrees Fahrenheit), and the coldest region is the northeast, where the average temperature is about 6 degrees Celsius (42.8 degrees Fahrenheit). The highest temperature ever recorded in Poland was 40.2 degrees Celsius (104.4 degrees Fahrenheit) in Prószków in 2023, and the lowest temperature ever recorded was -41 degrees Celsius (-41.8 degrees Fahrenheit) in Siedlce in 1940. The average annual precipitation is about 600 millimeters (23.6 inches), but it also varies depending on the region and the altitude. The wettest region is the mountains, where the average precipitation is about 1,200 millimeters (47.2 inches), and the driest region is the central lowlands, where the average precipitation is about 500 millimeters

(19.7 inches). The most common types of precipitation are rain, snow, and hail.

Poland's geography, climate, history, and culture have shaped its wildlife in various ways. Poland's location at the crossroads of different biogeographical regions has resulted in a high diversity of species and habitats. Poland's climate, with its four seasons and varying precipitation, has created different ecological niches and adaptations for its animals. Poland's history, with its periods of wars and partitions, has affected the distribution and conservation of its wildlife. Poland's culture, with its respect and appreciation for nature, has fostered a sense of responsibility and stewardship for its wildlife.

In this book, I will take you on a journey through the wildlife of Poland, and show you the wonders and challenges that it faces. I hope that you will enjoy reading this book as much as I enjoyed writing it, and that you will learn something new and interesting about the animals of Poland. I also hope that you will be inspired to visit Poland and see its wildlife for yourself, or to support its conservation efforts in any way you can.

Here is a map of Poland and its regions

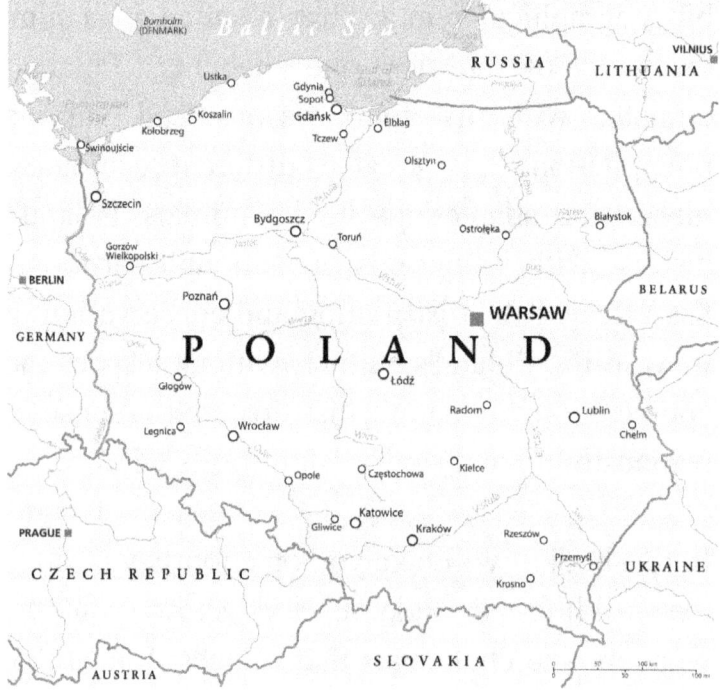

Chapter 1

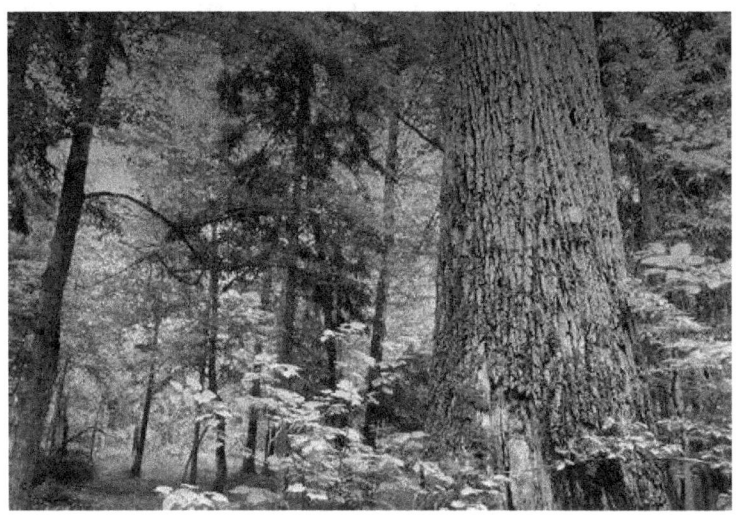

The Białowieża Forest: The Last Primeval Forest in Europe

The Białowieża Forest is a large forest complex located on the border between Poland and Belarus. It is one of the last and largest remaining parts of the immense primeval forest that once stretched across the European Plain. The forest is home to 800 European bison,

Europe's heaviest land animal, and many other rare and remarkable species of plants and animals. The forest is also a UNESCO World Heritage Site and a Biosphere Reserve, recognized for its outstanding natural and cultural values. In this chapter, we will explore the location, size, history, and importance of the Białowieża Forest, as well as the threats and challenges it faces, and the conservation efforts to protect it.

Location and size

The Białowieża Forest covers an area of about 3,085.8 square kilometers (1,191.4 square miles), of which 1,771.3 square kilometers (683.9 square miles) are in Poland and 1,314.5 square kilometers (507.5 square miles) are in Belarus. The forest straddles the watershed of the Baltic Sea and the Black Sea, and is crossed by several rivers, such as the Narewka, the

Hwoźna, and the Lesnaya. The forest is situated in the lowland region of the North European Plain, with an average altitude of about 150 meters (490 feet) above sea level. The highest point in the forest is Mount Dzerzhinskaya, at 346 meters (1,135 feet) above sea level, located in Belarus. The lowest point is the valley of the Narew River, at 90 meters (300 feet) above sea level, located in Poland.

The forest is divided into 16 administrative regions, called voivodeships in Poland and oblasts in Belarus. The Polish part of the forest belongs to the Podlaskie Voivodeship, and is subdivided into three counties: Hajnówka, Bielsk Podlaski, and Siemiatycze. The Belarusian part of the forest belongs to the Brest and Grodno Oblasts, and is subdivided into four districts: Kamenets, Pruzhany, Svislach, and Zelva. The forest also includes several towns and villages, such as Białowieża, Białowieża, and Kamieniuki in Poland, and Kamenyuki, Belaya Vezha, and Zalesye in Belarus.

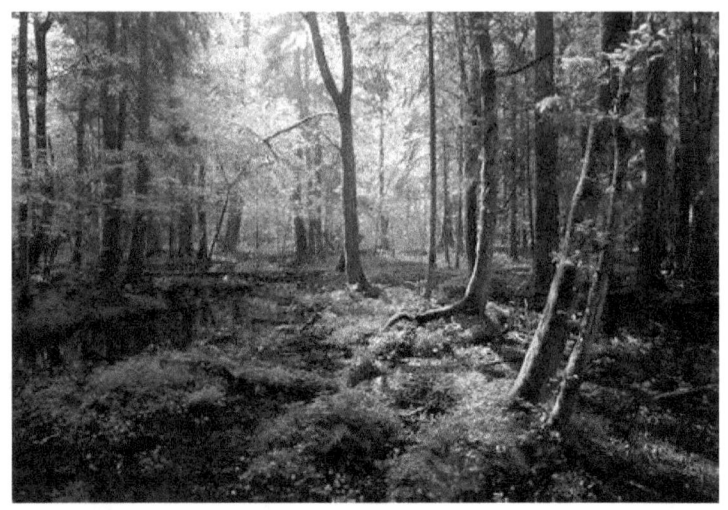

The forest is accessible by road, rail, and air. The nearest major cities are Białystok in Poland, about 62 kilometers (39 miles) northwest of the forest, and Brest in Belarus, about 70 kilometers (43 miles) south of the forest. The nearest airports are Warsaw Chopin Airport in Poland, about 230 kilometers (140 miles) west of the forest, and Minsk National Airport in Belarus, about 340 kilometers (210 miles) east of the forest. The nearest railway stations are Hajnówka in Poland, about 17 kilometers (11 miles) west of the forest, and Brest in Belarus, about 60 kilometers (37 miles) south of the forest. The forest is also connected by several roads, such as the national road 689 in Poland and the regional road P-80 in Belarus. There is a border crossing between Poland and Belarus in the forest, available for hikers and cyclists.

History and importance

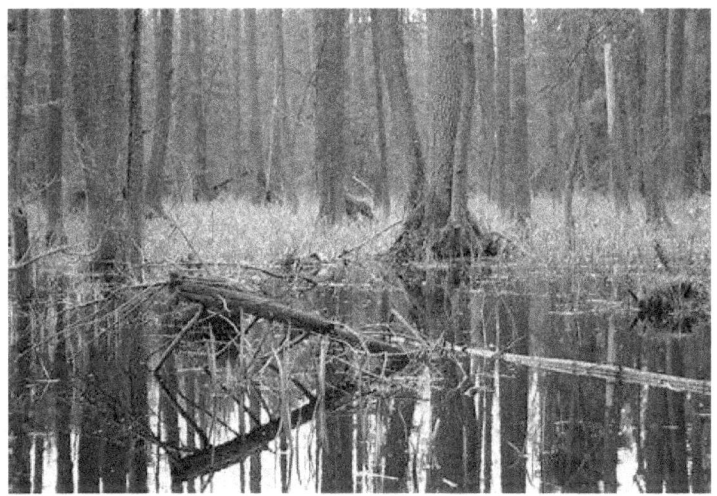

The Białowieża Forest has a long and complex history, marked by periods of glory and tragedy. The forest has witnessed the rise and fall of empires, the wars and invasions of different nations, and the changes and challenges of different eras. The forest has also been a source of inspiration and fascination for many people, such as kings and nobles, scientists and artists, and tourists and locals. The forest has also been a place of refuge and resistance for many people, such as partisans and rebels, hermits and outlaws, and Jews and Christians. The forest has also been a site of conflict and controversy for many people, such as loggers and conservationists, hunters and activists, and politicians and citizens.

The history of the Białowieża Forest can be traced back to the end of the last Ice Age, about 12,000 years ago, when the forest began to form from the tundra and the steppe. The first human settlements in the forest date back to the Neolithic period, about 6,000 years ago, when the forest was inhabited by the Corded Ware culture. The forest was later inhabited by various tribes and peoples, such as the Balts, the Slavs, the Vikings, the Mongols, and the Teutonic Knights. The forest became part of the Grand Duchy of Lithuania in the 14th century, and later part of the Polish-Lithuanian Commonwealth in the 16th century. The forest was then a royal hunting ground, where the kings and nobles enjoyed hunting the European bison and other game. The forest was also a place of scientific and cultural interest, where the naturalists and artists studied and depicted the flora and fauna of the forest.

The forest was partitioned and annexed by the neighboring powers in the 18th and 19th centuries, such as Prussia, Russia, and Austria. The forest was then exploited and degraded by the logging and farming activities of the new rulers. The forest was also affected by the wars and revolutions of the 20th century, such as the First and Second World Wars, the Polish-Soviet War, the Polish-Belarusian War, and the Soviet-Polish War. The forest was then a battleground and a hiding place, where the soldiers and partisans fought and died, and where the Jews and Christians escaped and survived. The forest was also a place of destruction and restoration, where the animals and plants were killed and saved, and where the European bison was exterminated and reintroduced.

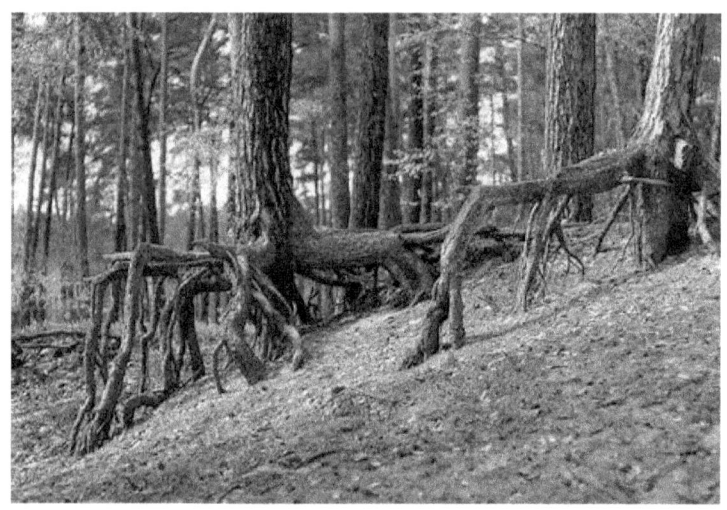

The forest became part of the People's Republic of Poland and the Soviet Union in the aftermath of the Second World War, and later part of the Republic of Poland and the Republic of Belarus after the collapse of the Soviet Union. The forest was then a protected area and a World Heritage Site, where the conservationists and managers worked and cooperated, and where the tourists and visitors admired and enjoyed. The forest was also a place of debate and dispute, where the environmentalists and developers argued and clashed, and where the local and national interests conflicted and compromised.

The importance of the Białowieża Forest is undeniable and undeniable. The forest is important for its ecological and biological values, as it is one of the largest and most intact temperate forests in Europe, and as it hosts a high diversity and abundance of species and habitats. The forest is important for its historical and cultural values, as it is a witness and a symbol of the past and present events and identities of the region, and as it is a source and a destination of the scientific and artistic endeavors and achievements of the people. The forest is important for its social and economic values, as it is a resource and a benefit for the livelihood and well-being of the local and global communities, and as it is a challenge and an opportunity for the development and conservation of the region.

The Białowieża Forest faces many threats and challenges that endanger its existence and integrity. The threats and challenges come from various sources and factors, such as natural and human-induced disturbances, climate change and invasive species, logging and hunting, and tourism and infrastructure. The threats and challenges have different impacts and consequences, such as habitat loss and fragmentation, species decline and extinction, ecosystem degradation and simplification, and cultural erosion and conflict. The threats and challenges require different responses and solutions, such as monitoring and research, legislation and management, restoration and protection, and education and awareness.

One of the main threats to the Białowieża Forest is the natural and human-induced disturbances, such as fire, wind, drought, and pests. These disturbances can affect the structure and function of the forest, by altering the composition and distribution of the trees and other plants, and by affecting the availability and quality of the resources and habitats for the animals and other organisms. The disturbances can also create opportunities and risks for the forest, by creating gaps and openings for the regeneration and succession of the forest, and by increasing the vulnerability and exposure of the forest to the other threats and challenges. The disturbances can also have positive and negative effects on the forest, by enhancing the diversity and resilience of the forest, and by reducing the biomass and carbon storage of the forest.

Another major threat to the Białowieża Forest is the climate change and invasive species, such as the rising temperature, the changing precipitation, and the alien plants and animals. These threats can affect the adaptation and survival of the forest, by altering the phenology and physiology of the trees and other plants, and by affecting the distribution and abundance of the animals and other organisms. These threats can also create shifts and changes for the forest, by altering the range and zone of the forest, and by affecting the interactions and dynamics of the forest. These threats can also have direct and indirect effects on the forest, by affecting the growth and productivity of the forest, and by affecting the services and functions of the forest.

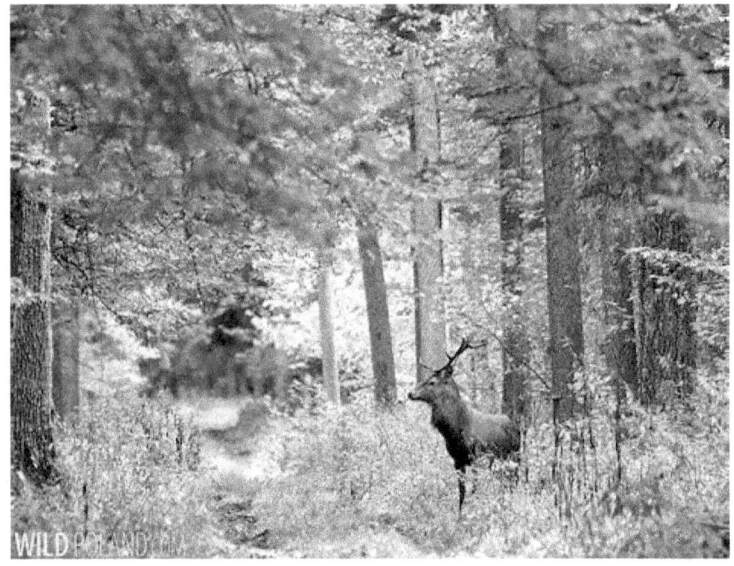

A further significant threat to the Białowieża Forest is the logging and hunting, such as the commercial and illegal harvesting of the trees and other plants, and the legal and poaching killing of the animals and other organisms. These threats can affect the diversity and richness of the forest, by reducing the number and variety of the trees and other plants, and by affecting the population and genetics of the animals and other organisms. These threats can also affect the balance and harmony of the forest, by disrupting the natural cycles and processes of the forest, and by affecting the relationships and roles of the forest.

Conservation efforts

The Białowieża Forest is protected by various national and international laws and agreements, such as the Polish Nature Conservation Act, the Belarusian Law on Specially Protected Natural Areas, the Ramsar Convention, the Bern Convention, the EU Habitats Directive, and the UNESCO World Heritage Convention. These laws and agreements aim to preserve and enhance the natural and cultural values of the forest, and to promote the sustainable use and management of the forest.

The forest is also managed by various national and local authorities and organizations, such as the Polish State Forests, the Belarusian Ministry of Forestry, the Białowieża National Park, the Belavezhskaya Pushcha National Park, the Białowieża Biosphere Reserve, the Biełavieżskaja Pušča Biosphere Reserve, and the Białowieża Forest World Heritage Site. These authorities and organizations work together to implement and monitor the conservation and restoration measures for the forest, and to coordinate and cooperate with the stakeholders and communities of the forest.

The forest is also supported by various international and non-governmental organizations and initiatives, such as the European Commission, the UNESCO, the

IUCN, the WWF, the Greenpeace, and the Save Białowieża Forest campaign. These organizations and initiatives provide funding and expertise for the conservation and research projects for the forest, and advocate and campaign for the protection and recognition of the forest.

Flora and fauna

The Białowieża Forest is one of the most biodiverse and rich areas in Europe, hosting more than 20,000 species of plants and animals. The forest is characterised by a mosaic of different types of forests, such as mixed deciduous, coniferous, riparian, and swamp forests, as well as meadows, marshes, bogs, and ponds. The forest is also distinguished by the presence of old-growth trees, some of which are more than 500 years old, and by the abundance of dead wood, which provides habitats and resources for many organisms.

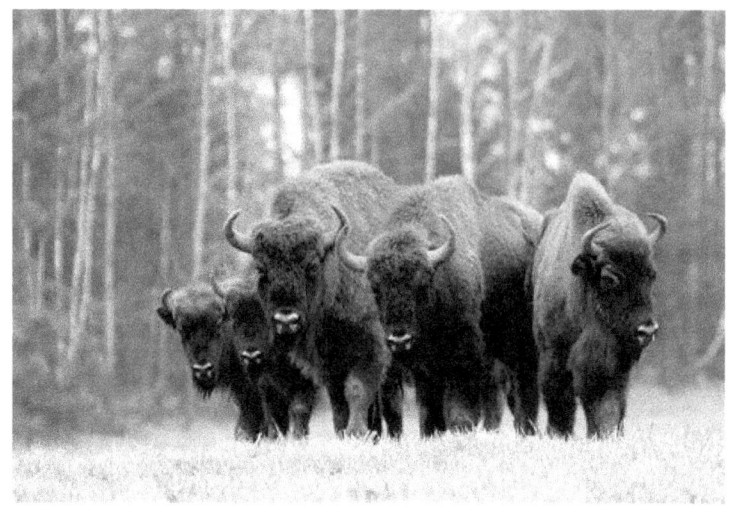

The forest is home to the European bison, the largest land mammal in Europe and one of Poland's national symbols. The European bison was once widespread across Europe, but was hunted to extinction in the wild by the early 20th century. The last wild bison in the Białowieża Forest was killed in 1919. Thanks to the captive breeding and reintroduction programs, the bison was restored to the wild in the 1950s, and now there are about 800 bison living in the forest, divided into two herds: one in the Polish part and one in the Belarusian part. The bison is a herbivore, feeding mainly on grasses, herbs, and twigs. The bison is a social animal, living in groups of 10 to 20 individuals, led by a dominant male. The bison is a keystone species, playing an important role in shaping and maintaining the forest ecosystem.

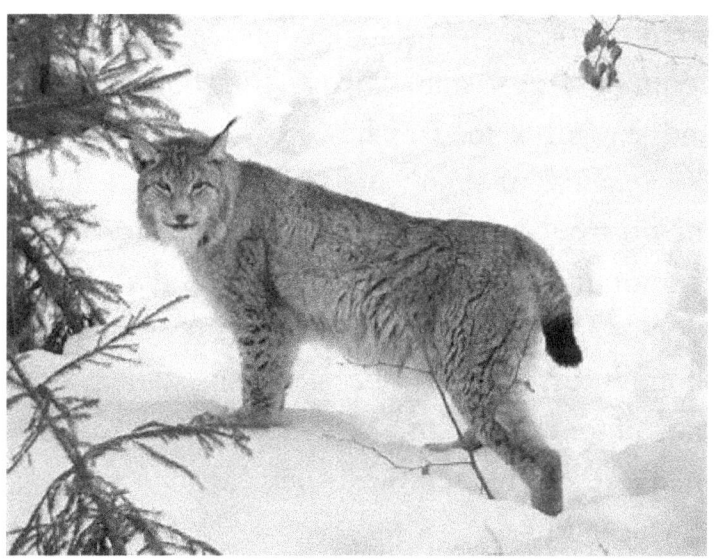

The forest is also home to many other mammals, such as wolves, lynxes, bears, wild boars, red deer, roe deer, elks, foxes, badgers, otters, beavers, martens, weasels, squirrels, dormice, hares, hedgehogs, bats, and rodents. The forest hosts more than 250 species of birds, such as white-tailed eagles, black storks, cranes, great bustards, black grouse, capercaillies, eagle owls, woodpeckers, warblers, thrushes, finches, and crossbills. The forest hosts more than 60 species of reptiles and amphibians, such as grass snakes, adders, slow worms, sand lizards, green lizards, pond turtles, fire salamanders, alpine newts, common frogs, marsh frogs, fire-bellied toads, and spadefoot toads. The forest hosts more than 70 species of fish, such as Atlantic salmon, brown trout, grayling, carp, pike, perch, zander, and minnows. The forest hosts more than 12,000 species of insects, such as butterflies, dragonflies, beetles, bees, wasps, ants, flies, mosquitoes, and spiders. The forest also hosts many other invertebrates, such as snails, worms, mites, and ticks.

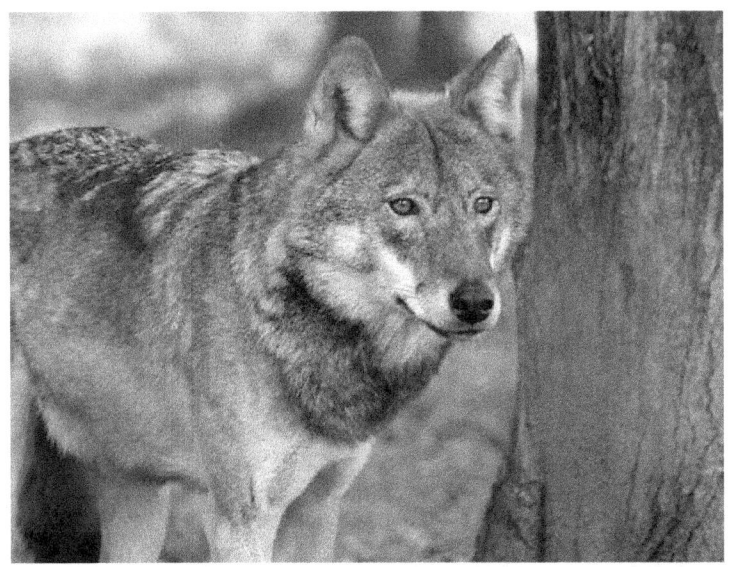

The Białowieża Forest is a treasure trove of life, a living museum of nature, and a window into the past. It is a forest that deserves our respect and admiration, our care and protection, and our visit and exploration.

Chapter 2

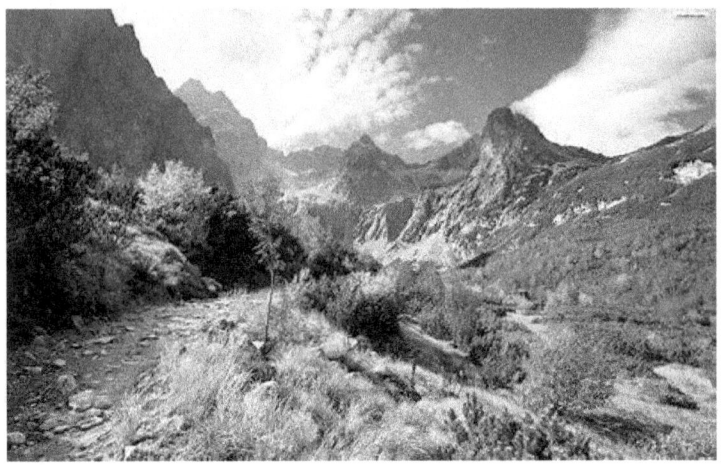

The Tatra Mountains: The Roof of Poland

The Tatra Mountains are the highest and most spectacular range of the Carpathian Mountains, a mountain chain that stretches across several countries in Central and Eastern Europe. The Tatra Mountains form a natural border between Poland and Slovakia, and are a popular tourist destination for both countries. The Tatra

Mountains are renowned for their scenic beauty, diverse landscapes, and rich wildlife. In this chapter, we will explore the location, size, history, and importance of the Tatra Mountains, as well as the different zones and habitats of the mountains, and how they change with the seasons and altitude. We will also highlight the unique and endemic species that live in the mountains, such as the Tatra chamois, the marmot, the bear, the eagle, the falcon, and the lynx. We will also include facts of other animals that live in the mountains, such as elks, otters, foxes, and more.

Location and size

The Tatra Mountains cover an area of about 785 square kilometers (303 square miles), of which about 525 square kilometers (203 square miles) are in Slovakia and about 260 square kilometers (100 square miles) are in Poland. The mountains extend for about 80 kilometers (50 miles) from east to west, and vary in width from 10 to 19 kilometers (6 to 12 miles) from north to south. The mountains are divided into two main parts: the Western Tatras and the Eastern Tatras, separated by the Chochołowska Valley in Poland and the Žiarska Valley in Slovakia. The Eastern Tatras are further subdivided into the High Tatras and the Belianske Tatras, separated by the Lendak Valley in Slovakia.

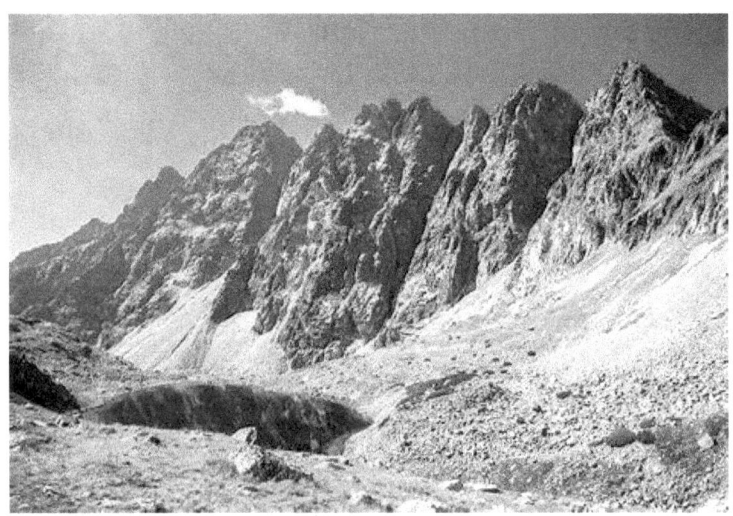

The Tatra Mountains are the highest range of the Carpathian Mountains, with 29 peaks above 2,500 meters (8,200 feet) and 10 peaks above 2,600 meters (8,500 feet). The highest peak of the Tatra Mountains, and of the entire Carpathian Mountains, is Gerlachovský štít, at 2,655 meters (8,710 feet), located in Slovakia. The highest peak of the Tatra Mountains in Poland, and the second highest peak of the entire range, is Rysy, at 2,499 meters (8,199 feet), located on the border with Slovakia. The lowest point of the Tatra Mountains is the valley of the Czarny Dunajec River, at 585 meters (1,919 feet), located in Poland.

The Tatra Mountains are accessible by road, rail, and air. The nearest major cities are Kraków in Poland, about 100 kilometers (62 miles) north of the mountains, and Poprad in Slovakia, about 15 kilometers (9 miles) south of the mountains. The nearest airports are Kraków-Balice Airport in Poland, about 120 kilometers (75 miles) north of the mountains, and Poprad-Tatry Airport in Slovakia, about 10 kilometers (6 miles) south of the mountains. The nearest railway stations are Zakopane in Poland, about 10 kilometers (6 miles) north of the mountains, and Poprad in Slovakia, about 15 kilometers (9 miles) south of the mountains. The mountains are also connected by several roads, such as the national road 47 in Poland and the state road 537 in Slovakia. There are several border crossings between Poland and Slovakia in the mountains, available for hikers and cyclists.

History and importance

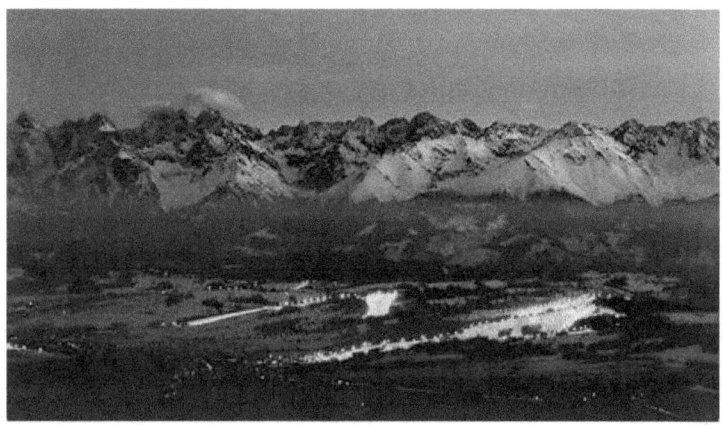

The Tatra Mountains have a long and complex history, marked by periods of exploration and exploitation, isolation and integration, and conflict and cooperation. The mountains have witnessed the rise and fall of civilizations, the migrations and invasions of peoples, and the changes and challenges of times. The mountains have also been a source of inspiration and fascination for many people, such as explorers and travelers, scientists and artists, and pilgrims and hermits. The mountains have also been a place of refuge and resistance for many people, such as rebels and partisans, minorities and exiles, and dissidents and activists. The mountains have also been a site of development and conservation for many people, such as settlers and farmers, loggers and miners, and tourists and managers.

The history of the Tatra Mountains can be traced back to the Paleolithic period, about 20,000 years ago, when the mountains were inhabited by the first human groups, such as the Aurignacian and the Gravettian cultures. The mountains were later inhabited by various tribes and peoples, such as the Celts, the Romans, the Germanic tribes, the Slavs, the Hungarians, and the Mongols. The mountains became part of the

Kingdom of Poland in the 10th century, and later part of the Polish-Lithuanian Commonwealth in the 16th century. The mountains were then a frontier and a borderland, where the Polish and Slovak cultures and languages met and mingled, and where the Catholic and Orthodox faiths coexisted and conflicted.

The mountains were partitioned and annexed by the neighboring powers in the 18th and 19th centuries, such as Austria, Prussia, and Russia. The mountains were then exploited and degraded by the industrial and agricultural activities of the new rulers. The mountains were also affected by the wars and revolutions of the 20th century, such as the First and Second World Wars, the Polish-Soviet War, the Slovak National Uprising, and the Velvet Revolution. The mountains were then a battleground and a hiding place, where the soldiers and partisans fought and died, and where the Jews and Roma escaped and survived. The mountains were also a place of destruction and restoration, where the forests and wildlife were damaged and protected, and where the Tatra chamois was hunted and reintroduced.

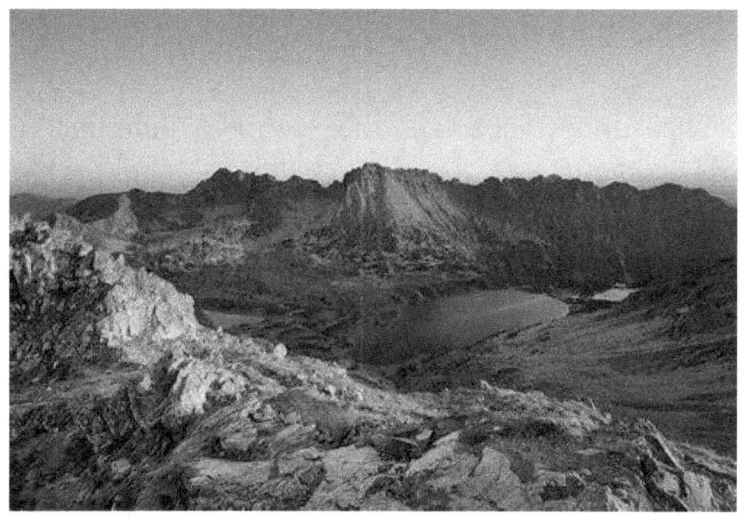

The mountains became part of the Republic of Poland and the Slovak Republic in the aftermath of the Second World War, and later part of the European Union in the early 21st century. The mountains were then a protected area and a tourist destination, where the conservationists and managers worked and cooperated, and where the visitors and locals admired and enjoyed. The mountains were also a place of debate and dispute, where the environmentalists and developers argued and clashed, and where the national and regional interests conflicted and compromised.

The importance of the Tatra Mountains is undeniable and undeniable. The mountains are important for their ecological and geological values, as they are the highest and most diverse range of the Carpathian Mountains, and as they host a high diversity and endemism of species and habitats. The mountains are important for their historical and cultural values, as they are a witness and a symbol of the past and present events and identities of the region, and as they are a source and a destination of the scientific and artistic endeavors and achievements of the people. The mountains are important for their social and economic values, as they are a resource and a benefit for the livelihood and well-being of the local and global communities, and as they are a challenge and an opportunity for the development and conservation of the region.

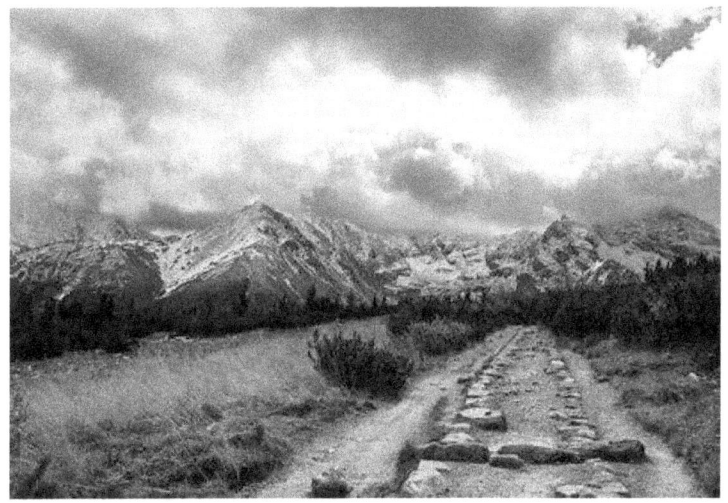

The Tatra Mountains are characterised by a
vertical zonation of different types of vegetation
and climate, which create different habitats and
ecosystems for the plants and animals. The
zonation is influenced by the altitude, the slope,
the exposure, and the soil of the mountains. The
zonation changes with the seasons, as the
temperature, the precipitation, and the daylight
vary throughout the year. The zonation can be

divided into four main zones: the foothill zone, the montane zone, the subalpine zone, and the alpine zone.

The foothill zone is the lowest and warmest zone of the mountains, ranging from 500 to 900 meters (1,600 to 3,000 feet) above sea level. The foothill zone is dominated by deciduous forests, mainly composed of beech, oak, hornbeam, and maple trees. The foothill zone is also interspersed with meadows, fields, orchards, and villages. The foothill zone has a temperate climate, with an average annual temperature of about 7 degrees Celsius (45 degrees Fahrenheit), and an average annual precipitation of about 800 millimeters (31 inches). The foothill zone is the most populated and cultivated zone of the mountains, and also the most affected by human activities, such as logging, farming, and urbanization.

The montane zone is the intermediate and transitional zone of the mountains, ranging from 900 to 1,400 meters (3,000 to 4,600 feet) above sea level. The montane zone is dominated by mixed forests, mainly composed of spruce, fir, pine, and larch trees. The montane zone is also interspersed with clearings, pastures, and chalets. The montane zone has a cool climate, with an average annual temperature of about 4 degrees Celsius (39 degrees Fahrenheit), and an average annual precipitation of about 1,000 millimeters (39 inches). The montane zone is the most visited and exploited zone of the mountains, and also the most vulnerable to natural disturbances, such as fire, wind, and pests.

The subalpine zone is the highest and coldest zone of the mountains, ranging from 1,400 to 1,800 meters (4,600 to 5,900 feet) above sea level. The subalpine zone has a cold climate, with an average annual temperature of about 1 degree Celsius (34 degrees Fahrenheit), and an average annual precipitation of about 1,200 millimeters (47.2 inches). The subalpine zone is the most exposed and windy zone of the mountains, and also the most snowy and frosty zone of the mountains.

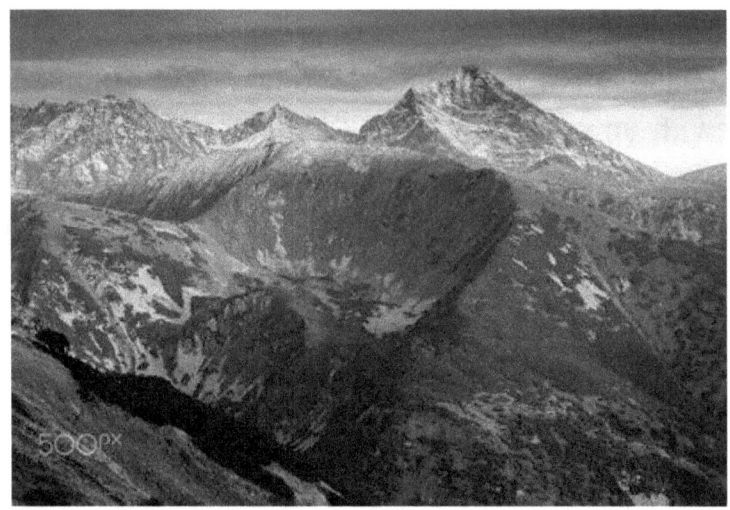

The alpine zone is the highest and most extreme zone of the mountains, ranging from 1,800 to 2,655 meters (5,900 to 8,710 feet) above sea level. The alpine zone is dominated by rocks, snow, and ice, with only a few patches of grasses and mosses. The alpine zone is also interspersed with glaciers, moraines, and tarns. The alpine zone has a polar climate, with an average annual temperature of about -6 degrees Celsius (21 degrees Fahrenheit), and an average annual precipitation of about 1,500 millimeters (59 inches). The alpine zone is the most isolated and inaccessible zone of the mountains, and also the most dangerous and challenging zone of the mountains.

Flora and fauna

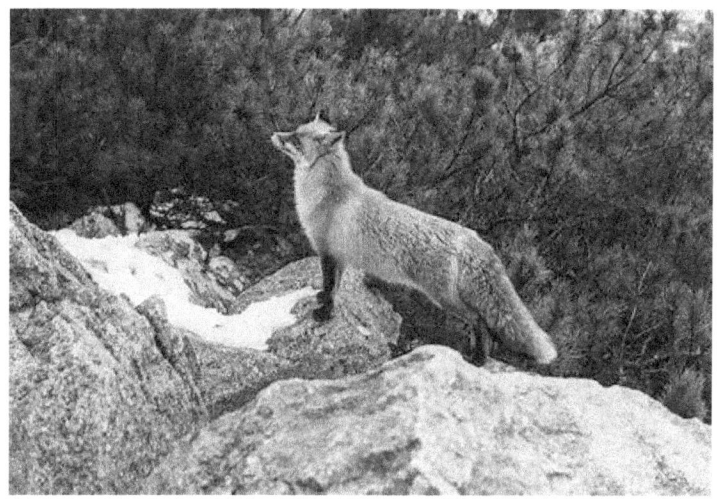

The Tatra Mountains are one of the most biodiverse and rich areas in Europe, hosting more than 10,000 species of plants and animals.

The mountains are characterised by a high degree of endemism, with many species that are unique to the Tatra Mountains or to the Carpathian Mountains. The mountains are also distinguished by the presence of relict species that survived the Ice Age in the Tatra Mountains or migrated from other regions after the Ice Age.

The mountains are home to the Tatra chamois, a subspecies of the Alpine chamois, and one of the symbols of the Tatra Mountains. The Tatra chamois is endemic to the Tatra Mountains, and is the only wild goat in Poland. The Tatra chamois lives in the subalpine and alpine zones of the mountains, where it feeds on grasses, herbs, and lichens. The Tatra chamois is a social animal, living in groups of 5 to 20 individuals, led by a dominant male. The Tatra chamois is a vulnerable species, threatened by poaching, habitat loss, and climate change.

The mountains are also home to many other mammals, such as bears, wolves, lynxes, wildcats, foxes, badgers, otters, martens,

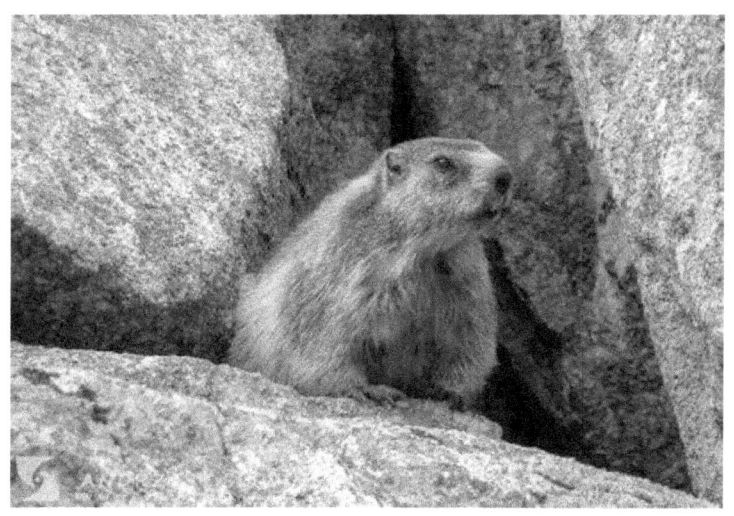

weasels, squirrels, marmots, dormice, hares, bats, and rodents. The mountains host more than 200 species of birds, such as golden eagles, peregrine falcons, eagle owls, pygmy owls, nutcrackers, wallcreepers, alpine accentors, snow finches, and white-winged snowfinches. The mountains host more than 30 species of reptiles and amphibians, such as vipers, smooth snakes, common lizards, alpine newts, fire salamanders, common toads, and common frogs. The mountains host more than 50 species of fish, such as brown trout, brook trout, grayling, minnows, and bullheads. The mountains host more than 5,000 species of insects, such as butterflies, moths, beetles, bees, wasps, ants, flies, mosquitoes, and spiders. The mountains also host many other invertebrates, such as snails, worms, mites, and ticks.

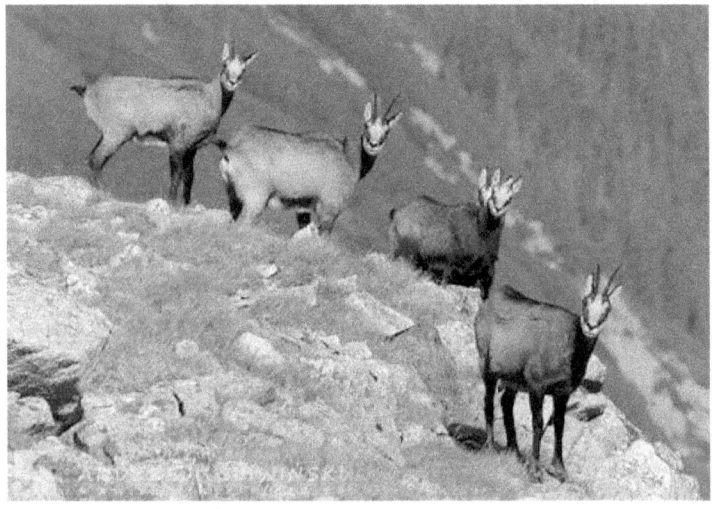

The Tatra Mountains are a mountain range that deserves our respect and admiration, our care and protection, and our visit and exploration.

Chapter 3

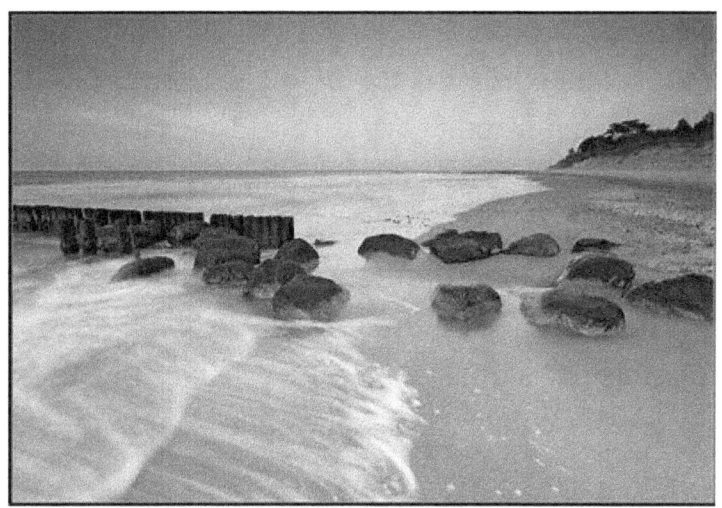

The Baltic Coast: The Land of the Sea Eagles

The Baltic Coast is a long and diverse shoreline that stretches from Germany to Russia, along the Baltic Sea, one of the largest brackish water bodies in the world. The Baltic Coast is a region of natural beauty, cultural diversity, and historical significance. The Baltic Coast is also a habitat for many rare and remarkable species of plants and animals, especially the white-tailed eagle, the largest bird of prey in Europe and another national symbol of Poland. In this chapter, we will explore the location, size, history, and importance of the Baltic Coast, as well as the different types of coastal landscapes, such as sandy beaches, dunes, cliffs, lagoons, and wetlands, and how they support various ecosystems and wildlife. We will also highlight the unique and endemic species that live on the coast, such as the white-tailed eagle, the seals, the porpoises, the storks, the cranes, and more.

Location and size

The Baltic Coast covers an area of about 93,000 square kilometers (36,000 square miles), and has a length of about 8,000 kilometers (5,000 miles). The Baltic Coast borders nine countries: Germany, Denmark, Sweden, Finland, Estonia, Latvia, Lithuania, Poland, and Russia. The Baltic Coast also includes several islands, such as Bornholm, Öland, Gotland, Åland, Saaremaa, and Hiiumaa. The Baltic Coast is divided into four main sections: the German Baltic Coast, the Scandinavian Baltic Coast, the Baltic States Coast, and the Polish-Russian Baltic Coast.

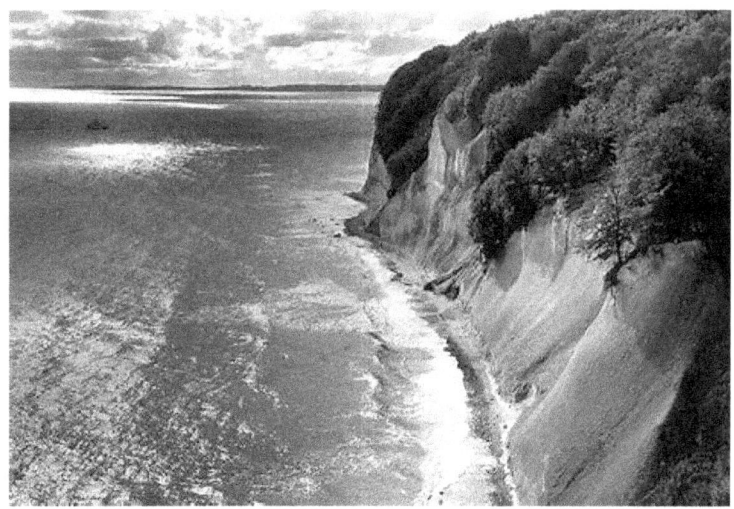

The German Baltic Coast extends from the mouth of the Elbe River to the border with Poland, and has a length of about 2,000 kilometers (1,200 miles). The German Baltic Coast is characterized by sandy beaches, dunes, cliffs, and lagoons, and is a popular tourist destination. The German Baltic Coast is also home to several national parks, such as the Jasmund National Park, the Western Pomerania

Lagoon Area National Park, and the Wadden Sea National Park.

The Scandinavian Baltic Coast extends from the border with Germany to the Gulf of Bothnia, and has a length of about 3,000 kilometers (1,900 miles). The Scandinavian Baltic Coast is characterized by rocky shores, archipelagos, and fjords, and is a region of scenic beauty and cultural diversity. The Scandinavian Baltic Coast is also home to several world heritage sites, such as the High Coast, the Kvarken Archipelago, and the Naval Port of Karlskrona.

The Baltic States Coast extends from the Gulf of Bothnia to the border with Russia, and has a length of about 1,500 kilometers (900 miles). The Baltic States Coast is characterised by sandy beaches, dunes, wetlands, and forests, and is a region of natural and historical interest. The Baltic States Coast is also home to several biosphere reserves, such as the West Estonian Archipelago, the North Vidzeme, and the Nemunas Delta.

The Polish-Russian Baltic Coast extends from the border with Lithuania to the border with Finland, and has a length of about 1,500 kilometers (900 miles). The Polish-Russian Baltic Coast is characterized by sandy beaches, dunes, cliffs, and lagoons, and is a region of economic and strategic importance. The Polish-Russian Baltic Coast is also home to several national parks, such as the Słowiński National Park, the Wolin National Park, and the Kurshskaya Kosa National Park.

History and importance

The Baltic Coast has a long and complex history, marked by periods of exploration and trade, colonization and conquest, and cooperation and conflict. The Baltic Coast has witnessed the rise and fall of civilizations, the migrations and invasions of peoples, and the changes and challenges of times. The Baltic Coast has also been a source of inspiration and fascination for many people, such as explorers and traders, scientists and artists, and pilgrims and hermits. The Baltic Coast has also been a place of refuge and resistance for many people, such as rebels and partisans, minorities and exiles, and dissidents and activists. The Baltic Coast has also been a site of development and conservation for many people, such as settlers and farmers, fishermen and sailors, and tourists and managers.

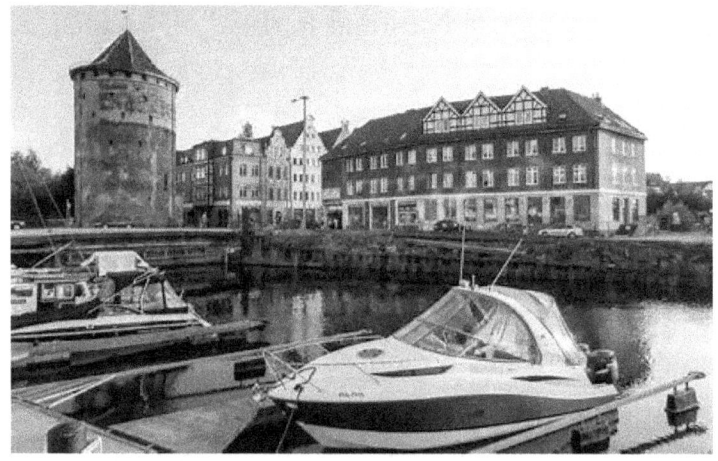

The history of the Baltic Coast can be traced back to the Stone Age, about 10,000 years ago, when the first human settlements appeared along the coast, after the retreat of the glaciers. The Baltic Coast was later inhabited by various tribes and peoples, such as the Germanic tribes, the Slavic tribes, the Vikings, the Teutonic Knights, and the Hanseatic League. The Baltic Coast became a region of maritime commerce and cultural exchange, as well as a region of territorial disputes and military conflicts.

The Baltic Coast was partitioned and annexed by the neighboring powers in the 17th and 18th centuries, such as Sweden, Russia, Prussia, and Denmark. The Baltic Coast was then a region of political and economic domination, as well as a region of cultural and religious oppression. The Baltic Coast was also affected by the wars and revolutions of the 19th and 20th centuries, such as the Napoleonic Wars, the Crimean War, the First and Second World Wars, the Baltic States' independence, and the Cold War. The Baltic Coast was then a region of strategic and ideological importance, as well as a region of destruction and suffering.

The Baltic Coast became part of the European Union in the late 20th and early 21st centuries, after the collapse of the Soviet Union and the reunification of Germany. The Baltic Coast is now a region of integration and cooperation, as well as a region of diversity and identity. The Baltic Coast is also a region of environmental and cultural protection, as well as a region of tourism and development.

The importance of the Baltic Coast is undeniable and undeniable. The Baltic Coast is important for its geographical and geopolitical values, as it is a long and diverse shoreline that connects the Baltic Sea with the North Sea and the Atlantic Ocean, and as it borders nine countries with different histories and cultures. The Baltic Coast is important for its historical and cultural values, as it is a witness and a symbol of the past and present events and identities of the region, and as it is a source and a destination of the scientific and artistic endeavors and achievements of the people. The Baltic Coast is important for its ecological and biological values, as it is a habitat for many rare and remarkable species of plants and animals, especially the white-tailed eagle, the largest bird of prey in Europe and another national symbol of Poland.

Coastal landscapes and ecosystems

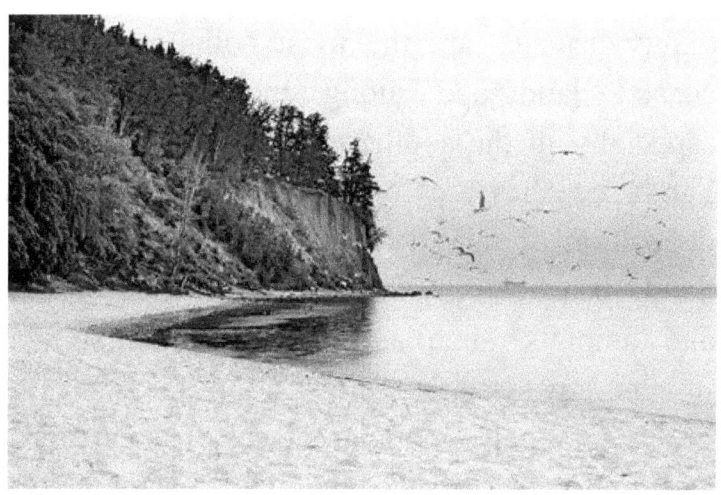

The Baltic Coast is characterized by a variety of coastal landscapes and ecosystems, such as sandy beaches, dunes, cliffs, lagoons, and wetlands, that support a rich and diverse flora and fauna. The coastal landscapes and ecosystems are influenced by the physical and chemical characteristics of the Baltic Sea, such as the salinity, the temperature, the currents, and the tides. The coastal landscapes and ecosystems also change with the seasons and the altitude, as the climate, the vegetation, and the wildlife vary throughout the year and along the coast.

Sandy beaches are the most common type of coastal landscape along the Baltic Coast, especially in the southern and eastern sections. Sandy beaches are formed by the erosion and deposition of sand by the waves and the wind. Sandy beaches provide habitats for many plants and animals, such as grasses, herbs, shrubs, insects, crustaceans, mollusks, and birds. Sandy beaches are also popular places for recreation and tourism, such as swimming, sunbathing, surfing, and sailing.

Dunes are the most distinctive type of coastal landscape along the Baltic Coast, especially in the northern and western sections. Dunes are formed by the accumulation and stabilization of sand by the wind and the vegetation. Dunes provide habitats for many plants and animals, such as lyme grass, sea buckthorn, juniper, rabbits, foxes, lizards, and birds. Dunes are also important places for conservation and protection, as they act as natural barriers against the sea erosion and the storm surges.

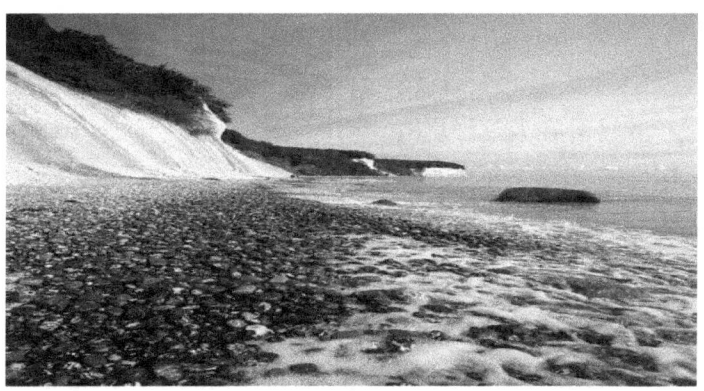

Cliffs are the most dramatic type of coastal landscape along the Baltic Coast, especially in the central and eastern sections. Cliffs are formed by the erosion and weathering of rocks by the waves and the wind. Cliffs provide habitats for many plants and animals, such as mosses, lichens, ferns, orchids, bats, rodents, raptors, and seabirds. Cliffs are also scenic places for observation and exploration, as they offer spectacular views and geological features.

Lagoons are the most diverse type of coastal landscape along the Baltic Coast, especially in the southern and eastern sections. Lagoons are formed by the separation of the sea by sandbars, spits, or islands. Lagoons have varying degrees of salinity, depending on the connection with the sea and the freshwater inflow. Lagoons provide habitats for many plants and animals, such as reeds, sedges, water lilies, fish, amphibians, reptiles, waterfowl, and waders. Lagoons are also valuable places for fishing and aquaculture, as they are rich in fish and shellfish resources.

Wetlands are formed by the flooding or saturation of land by water, either permanently or seasonally. Wetlands have various types, such as marshes, swamps, bogs, and fens. Wetlands provide habitats for many plants and animals, such as willows, alders, birches, cranberries, sundews, beavers, otters, frogs, snakes, storks, cranes, and ducks. Wetlands are also important places for water purification and regulation, as they filter and store water, and prevent floods and droughts. Wetlands are also valuable places for recreation and education, as they offer opportunities for birdwatching, fishing, and learning.

Flora and fauna

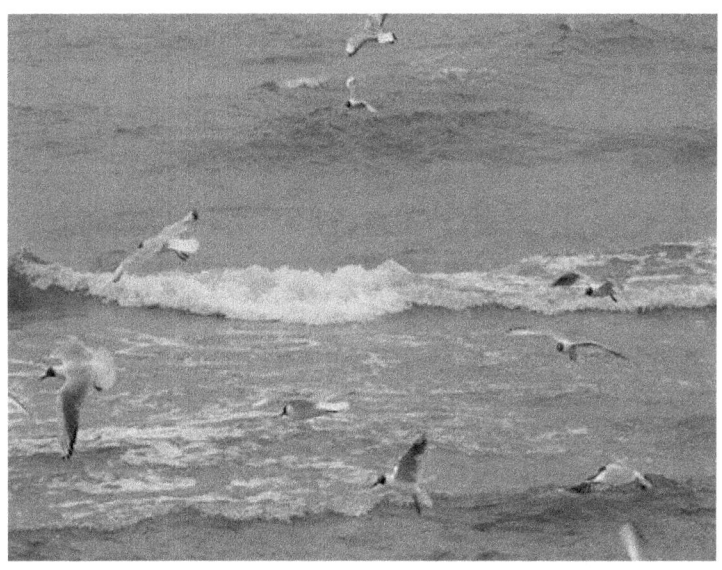

The Baltic Coast is one of the most biodiverse and rich areas in Europe, hosting more than 15,000 species of plants and animals. The coast is characterized by a high degree of endemism, with many species that are unique to the Baltic Coast or to the Baltic Sea. The coast is also distinguished by the presence of relict species, that survived the Ice Age in the Baltic Coast or migrated from other regions after the Ice Age.

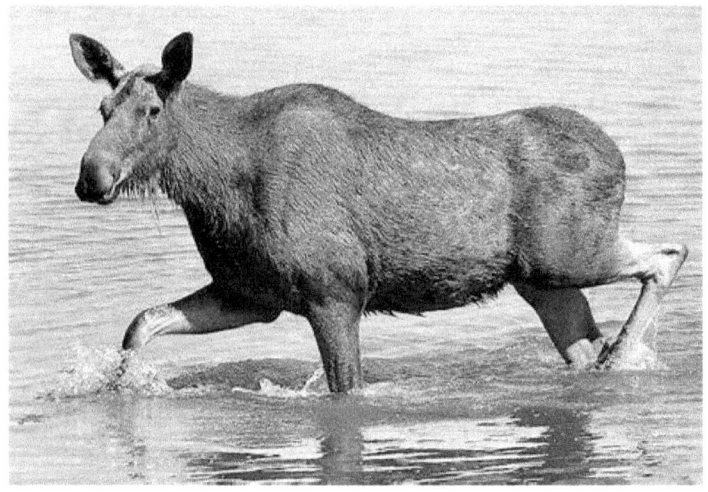

The coast is home to the white-tailed eagle, the largest bird of prey in Europe and another national symbol of Poland. The white-tailed eagle is a majestic and powerful raptor, with a wingspan of up to 2.4 meters (7.9 feet) and a weight of up to 7 kilograms (15 pounds). The white-tailed eagle lives on the cliffs and islands of the coast, where it builds large nests of sticks and branches. The white-tailed eagle feeds mainly on fish, but also on birds, mammals, and carrion. The white-tailed eagle is a monogamous and territorial animal, living in pairs that mate for life and defend their territory. The white-tailed eagle is a vulnerable species, threatened by habitat loss, pollution, and persecution.

The coast is also home to many other birds, such as seals, porpoises, storks, cranes, herons, gulls, terns, cormorants, and swans. The coast hosts more than 100 species of fish, such as cod, herring, salmon, eel, flounder, and perch. The coast hosts more than 1,000 species of invertebrates, such as crabs, shrimps, mussels, oysters, snails, worms, and jellyfish. The coast also hosts many other plants and animals, such as seaweeds, grasses, flowers, fungi, lichens, deer, foxes, hares, and rodents.

The Baltic Coast is a treasure trove of life, a living museum of nature, and a window into the past. It is a coast that deserves our respect and admiration, our care and protection, and our visit and exploration.

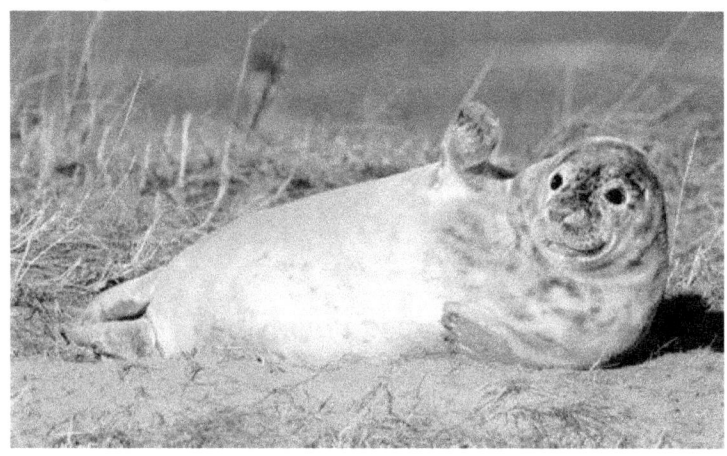

Chapter 4

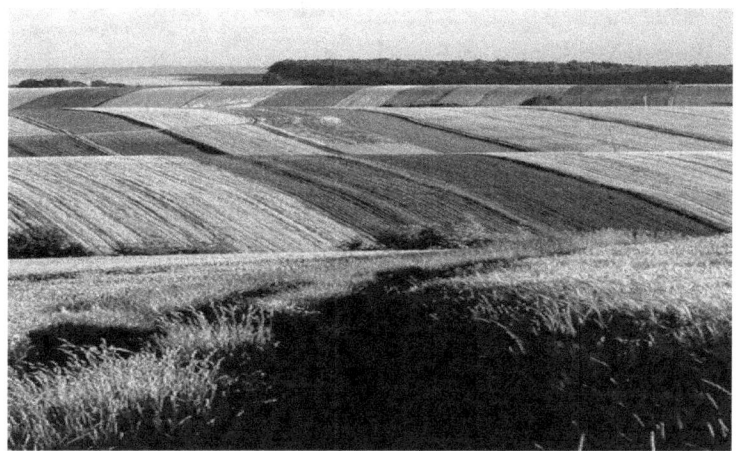

The Central Lowlands: The Heart of Poland

The Central Lowlands are a vast and fertile plain that covers most of Poland and is home to most of its population and agriculture. They are located in the center of Europe, between the Baltic Sea in the north and the Carpathian Mountains in the south. They have a long and rich history, dating back to the prehistoric times, when they were inhabited by various cultures and tribes. They are important for Poland's economy, culture, and identity, as they contain many historical and cultural landmarks, such as Warsaw, Krakow, and Gdansk. They are also important for Poland's biodiversity, as they provide habitats and resources for many animals, both common and rare.

Lowland Landscapes

- The Central Lowlands are composed of different types of landscapes, such as forests, meadows, fields, rivers, and lakes.
- Forests cover about 30% of the lowlands, mainly in the east and north. They are mostly deciduous, with oak, beech, birch, and hornbeam as the dominant species. Some of the forests are ancient and undisturbed, such as the Bialowieza Forest, which is a UNESCO World Heritage Site and the last refuge of the European bison[1].
- Meadows and fields cover about 60% of the lowlands, mainly in the west and south. They are

used for agriculture, mainly for growing cereals, potatoes, sugar beets, and rapeseed. They are also important for maintaining the rural landscape and the traditional way of life of the Polish farmers.

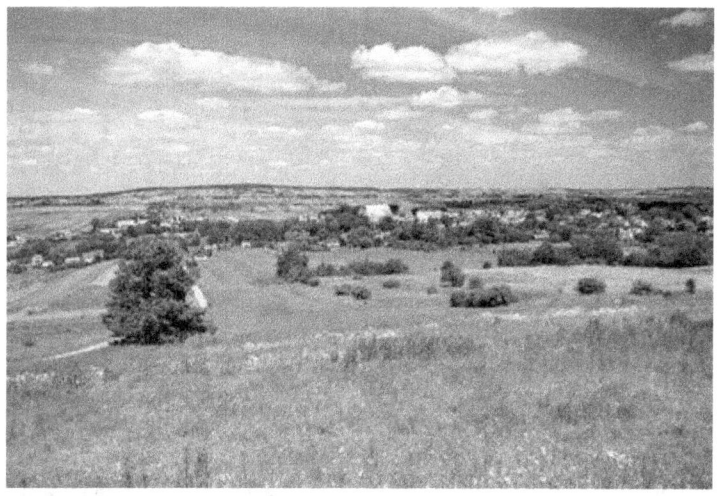

- Rivers and lakes are abundant in the lowlands, as they were formed by the melting of the glaciers during the last ice age. The main rivers are the Vistula, the Oder, the Warta, and the Bug, which flow into the Baltic Sea. The main lakes are the Masurian Lakes, the Pomeranian Lakes, and the Wielkopolska Lakes, which are popular tourist destinations for fishing, boating, and swimming.

Lowland Animals

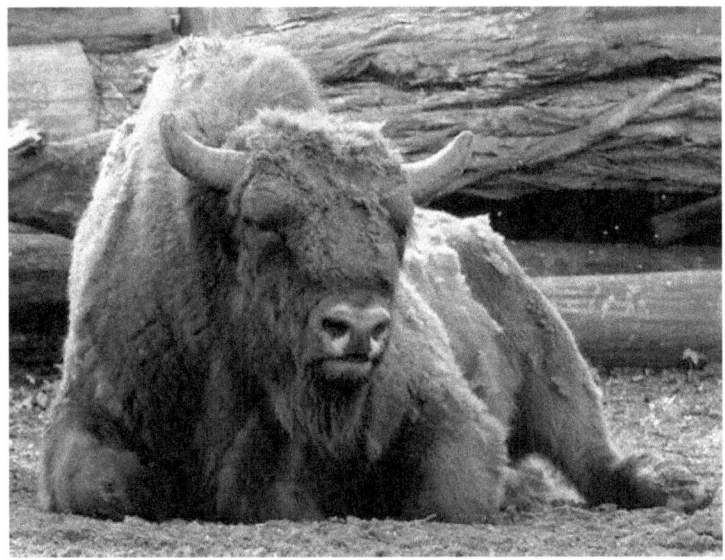

- The Central Lowlands are home to many animals, both common and rare, that depend on the diverse and rich lowland landscapes for their survival.
- Some of the common and familiar species that live in the lowlands are the deer, the boar, the

hare, the hedgehog, and the fox. They are mostly herbivorous or omnivorous, and they feed on the plants, fruits, seeds, and insects that are available in the forests, meadows, and fields.

- Some of the other animals that live in the lowlands are the bats, the frogs, the butterflies, and more. They are mostly nocturnal, aquatic, or aerial, and they feed on the nectar, pollen, worms, and fish that are available in the forests, rivers, and lakes.

- Some of the rare and endangered species that live in the lowlands are the European bison, the wolf, the lynx, and the crane. They are mostly carnivorous or omnivorous, and they feed on the deer, boar, hare, and other animals that are available in the forests, meadows, and fields. They are threatened by habitat loss, poaching, and human interference, and they are protected by law and conservation efforts.

The Central Lowlands are a vital part of Poland's geography, history, and culture, as they cover most of the country and host most of its people and activities. They are also a vital part of

Poland's ecology, as they host many animals, both common and rare, that rely on the diverse and rich lowland landscapes for their survival. They are a source of beauty, wealth, and pride for Poland, and they deserve to be respected, preserved, and appreciated..

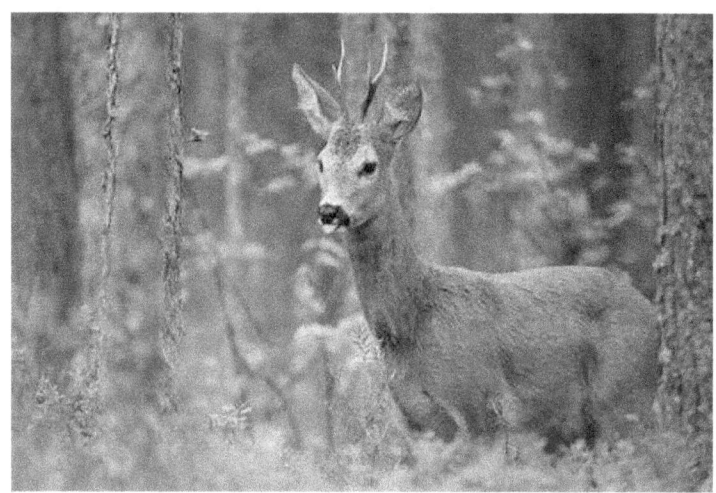

Chapter 5

The Future of Polish Wildlife: Challenges and Opportunities.

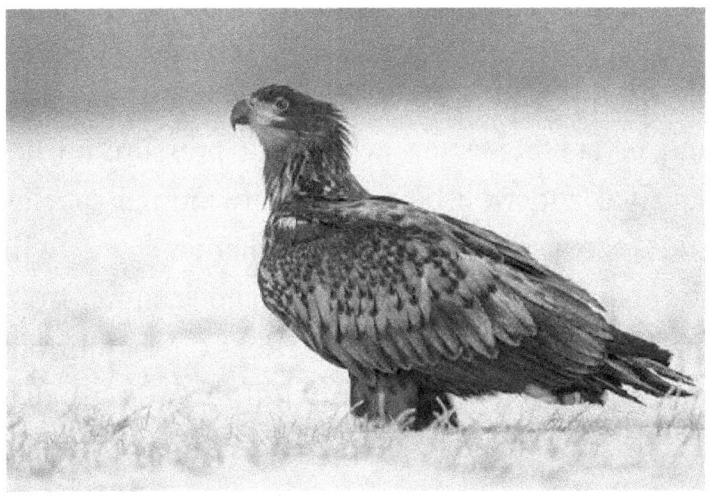

Poland is home to a vast array of wildlife, with some of the best spots for animal watching being the Biebrza Marshes, the Bialowieza Forest, and the Wisla River. Polish wildlife has undergone significant changes in the past decades, due to various social, economic, and environmental factors.

Some of these changes have been positive, such as the recovery of large carnivores like the wolf, the lynx, and the bear, thanks to legal protection and public awareness. However, many challenges and threats still remain, such as habitat loss, climate change, pollution, hunting, and invasive species, which put pressure on the survival and well-being of many animal species and ecosystems. In this chapter, we will summarise the main findings and insights from the previous chapters and reflect on the current state and trends of Polish wildlife. We will also discuss the main challenges and opportunities that Polish animals face in the future, and suggest some possible solutions and actions that can help conserve and enhance Polish wildlife.

Polish wildlife is rich and diverse, but also vulnerable and threatened by various factors. We can also observe that Polish wildlife has experienced significant changes over time, both positive and negative, due to natural and human influences. We can also appreciate that Polish wildlife is valuable and essential for the functioning of the environment and the well-being of humans.

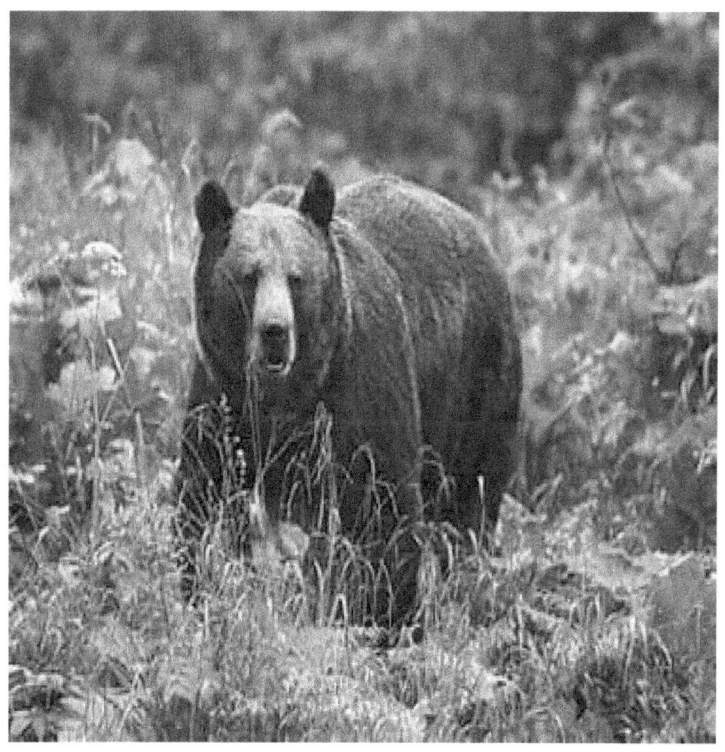

Looking ahead, Polish wildlife faces many challenges and opportunities in the future, which will determine its fate and prospects. Some of the main challenges and opportunities are:

Habitat loss: Habitat loss is one of the most serious threats to Polish wildlife, as it reduces the available space and resources for animals to live and thrive. Habitat loss is mainly caused by urbanisation, agriculture, forestry, infrastructure, and tourism, which fragment and degrade natural landscapes. Habitat loss affects different animal groups and regions differently, depending on their ecological needs and adaptability. For example, large carnivores like the wolf require large and connected habitats to maintain viable populations, while amphibians like the frog are sensitive to changes in water quality and availability. Habitat loss can also lead to other problems, such as human-wildlife conflicts, genetic isolation, and invasive species.

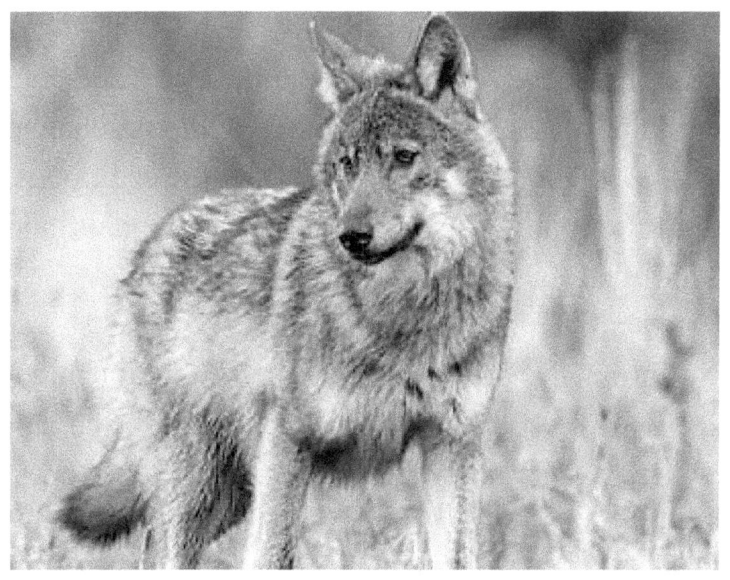

Climate change: Climate change is another major threat to Polish wildlife, as it alters the temperature, precipitation, and seasonality of the environment. Climate change can affect the distribution, abundance, and behavior of animal species, as well as the composition and functioning of ecosystems. Climate change can also exacerbate other threats, such as habitat loss, pollution, and diseases. For example, climate change can shift the range and phenology of migratory birds, such as the stork, which depend on the availability of food and nesting sites along their routes. Climate change can also increase the risk of wildfires, floods, and droughts, which can damage habitats and wildlife.

Pollution: Pollution is another significant threat to Polish wildlife, as it contaminates the air, water, and soil with harmful substances. Pollution can affect the health, reproduction, and survival of animal species, as well as the quality and productivity of ecosystems. Pollution can also interact with other factors, such as climate change, habitat loss, and invasive species, to create synergistic effects. For example, pollution can reduce the immunity and resistance of animals to diseases and parasites, such as the African swine fever that affects wild boars. Pollution can also reduce the availability and diversity of food sources for animals, such as the insects that feed on flowers and plants.

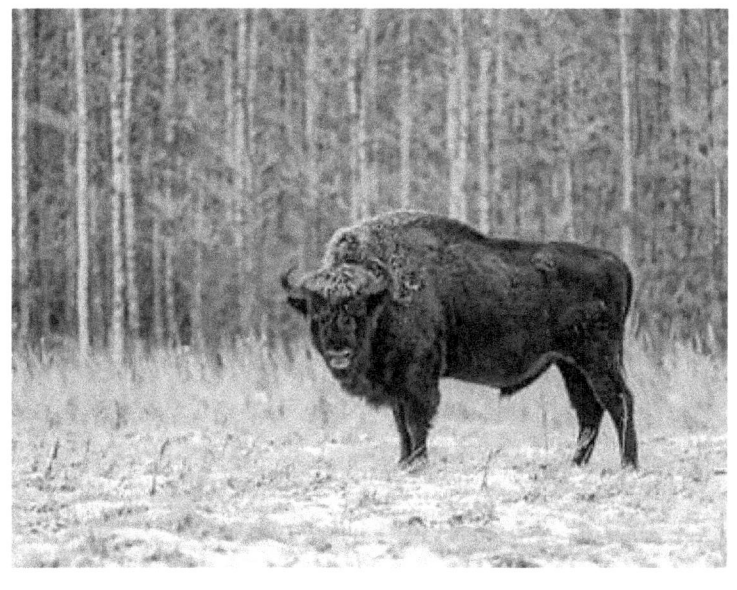

Hunting: Hunting is another important factor that influences Polish wildlife, as it directly affects the mortality and population dynamics of animal species. Hunting can have both positive and negative impacts on wildlife, depending on the species, the methods, and the regulations involved. Hunting can be a tool for wildlife management, conservation, and research, as well as a source of income, recreation, and culture for humans. However, hunting can also be a cause of wildlife decline, extinction, and conflict, especially when it is illegal, unsustainable, or unethical. For example, hunting can reduce the genetic diversity and viability of animal populations, such as the bison, which was nearly exterminated in the past[7]. Hunting can also increase the hostility and mistrust between hunters and non-hunters, as well as between humans and wildlife.

Invasive species: Invasive species are another challenge for Polish wildlife, as they are non-native species that have been introduced or spread to new areas, where they compete with or prey on native species, or alter the structure and function of ecosystems. Invasive species can affect different animal groups and regions differently, depending on their characteristics and impacts. For example, invasive species can reduce the diversity and abundance of native species, such as the raccoon dog, which competes with and transmits diseases to native carnivores[8]. Invasive species can also change the ecosystem processes and services, such as the

American mink, which reduces the water quality and vegetation of wetlands.

Despite these challenges, Polish wildlife also has many opportunities and solutions that can help conserve and enhance it in the future. Some of the main opportunities and solutions are:

Education: Education is one of the most effective and long-term solutions for Polish wildlife, as it can increase the knowledge, awareness, and appreciation of wildlife among the public, especially the younger generations. Education can also foster the values, attitudes, and behaviors that support wildlife conservation and coexistence, as well as the skills and competencies that enable wildlife protection and management. Education can take various forms and methods, such as formal, informal, and non-formal education, as well as experiential, participatory, and interactive education. For example, education can involve school curricula, field trips, workshops, campaigns, media, and social networks, among others.

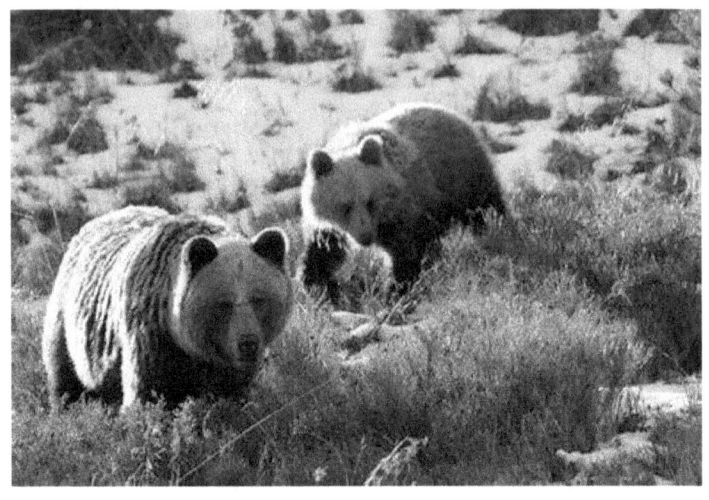

Research: Research is another vital and ongoing solution for Polish wildlife, as it can provide the scientific information, evidence, and innovation that are needed for wildlife conservation and management. Research can also contribute to the understanding, monitoring, and assessment of wildlife populations, habitats, and threats, as well as the evaluation and improvement of wildlife policies and practices. Research can involve various disciplines and approaches, such as biology, ecology, sociology, economics, and law, as well as interdisciplinary and transdisciplinary research. For example, research can involve surveys, experiments, models, databases, and indicators, among others.

Legislation: Legislation is another essential and powerful solution for Polish wildlife, as it can provide the legal framework, standards, and instruments that regulate and enforce wildlife conservation and management. Legislation can also reflect and influence the political will, public opinion, and international cooperation on wildlife issues, as well as the rights and responsibilities of different stakeholders and actors involved in wildlife. Legislation can include various levels and types, such as national, regional, and local laws, as well as international conventions and agreements. For example, legislation can involve the protection of species and habitats, the control of hunting and trade, and the prevention of pollution and climate change, among others.

Management: Management is another crucial and practical solution for Polish wildlife, as it can implement and coordinate the actions and measures that are necessary for wildlife conservation and management. Management can also adapt and respond to the changing conditions and challenges of wildlife, as well as the needs and expectations of humans. Management can involve various actors and sectors, such as government, non-government, and private organisations, as well as local communities and individuals. Management can also involve various tools and methods, such as planning, monitoring, evaluation, and communication. For example, management can involve the establishment and maintenance of protected areas, the compensation and mitigation of human-wildlife conflicts, and the promotion and support of wildlife tourism, among others.

Restoration: Restoration is another promising and beneficial solution for Polish wildlife, as it can restore and enhance the habitats and ecosystems that are degraded or destroyed by human activities. Restoration can also improve the quality and quantity of the resources and services that wildlife and humans depend on, as well as the resilience and diversity of wildlife and ecosystems. Restoration can involve various scales and techniques, such as landscape, ecosystem, and species restoration, as well as passive, active, and assisted restoration. For example, restoration can involve the reforestation of deforested areas, the reconnection of fragmented habitats, and the reintroduction of extirpated species, among others.

Chapter 6

Travel Tips For Wildlife Watching In Poland

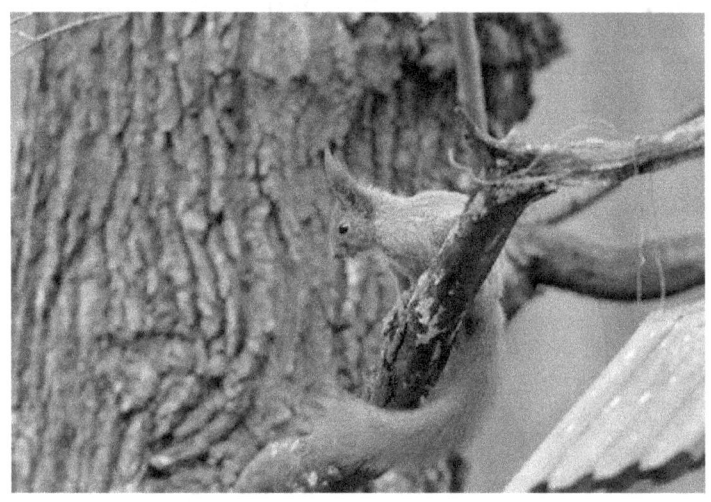

Poland is a great destination for wildlife enthusiasts, as it offers a variety of habitats and species to observe and admire. Whether you want to see the majestic European bison, the elusive lynx, the graceful white-tailed eagle, or the colourful black grouse, you will find plenty of opportunities to do so in Poland. However, you will need to plan your trip carefully, as different animals have different preferences and behaviours. Here are some tips to help you make the most of your wildlife safari in Poland:

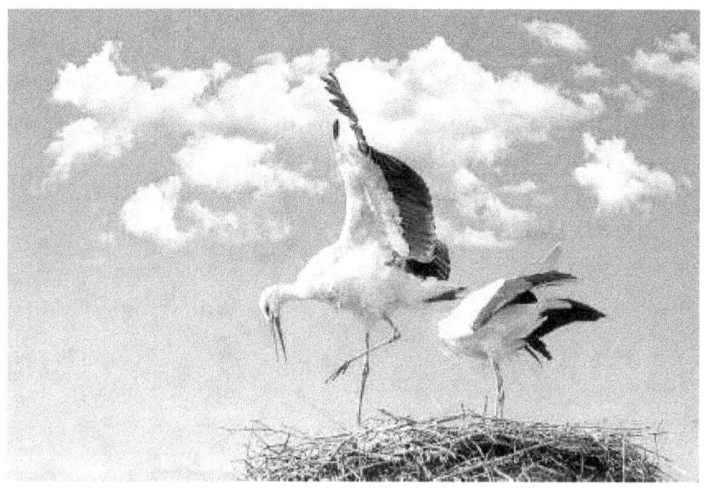

- Choose the best places to go: Poland has 23 national parks and 10 biosphere reserves that protect its natural heritage and biodiversity. Some of the best places for wildlife watching are the Biebrza Marshes, the Białowieża Forest, and the Wisła River. The Biebrza Marshes are the largest wetland complex in Europe, home to over 270 bird species, including the rare aquatic warbler, the white-winged black tern, and the great snipe. The Białowieża Forest is the last and largest remaining primeval forest on the European Plain, home to the largest population of European bison, as well as wolves, lynxes, bears, and woodpeckers. The Wisła River is the longest and largest river in Poland, home to a variety of fish, amphibians, reptiles, and mammals, including the beaver, the otter, and the European pond turtle.

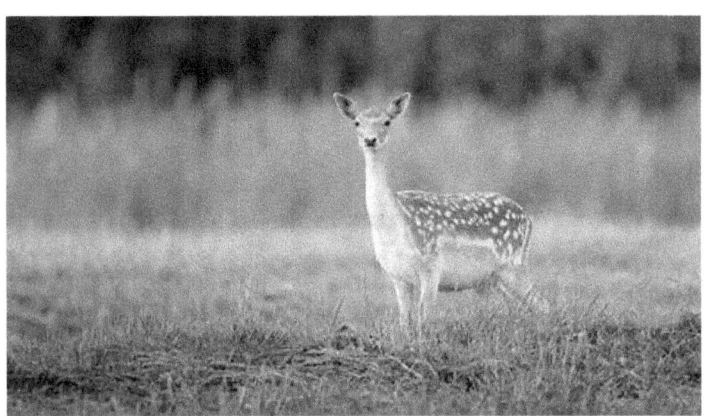

- Choose the best seasons and times to go: Depending on what animals you want to see, you will need to choose the appropriate season and time of day to visit. For example, if you want to see the bison, the best time is in winter, when they gather in open areas to feed and are easier to spot. If you want to see the lynx, the best time is in spring, when they are more active and vocal during the mating season. If you want to see the white-tailed eagle, the best time is in autumn, when they congregate along the rivers and lakes to feed on migrating fish. If you want to see the black grouse, the best time is in the early morning, when they perform their spectacular courtship display on the leks. Generally, the best times of day for wildlife watching are dawn and dusk, when most animals are more active and less disturbed by human presence.

- Choose the best equipment and precautions to take: To enjoy your wildlife safari in Poland, you will need to bring some essential equipment and take some necessary precautions. For example, you will need a good pair of binoculars or a spotting scope to observe the animals from a safe distance and avoid disturbing them. You will also need a camera or a smartphone to capture the memorable moments and share them with your friends and family. You will also need appropriate clothing and footwear to suit the weather and terrain conditions, as well as insect repellent and sunscreen to protect yourself from bites and burns. You will also need to follow some basic rules of wildlife watching, such as keeping quiet, staying on the trails, respecting the animals' space, and leaving no trace.

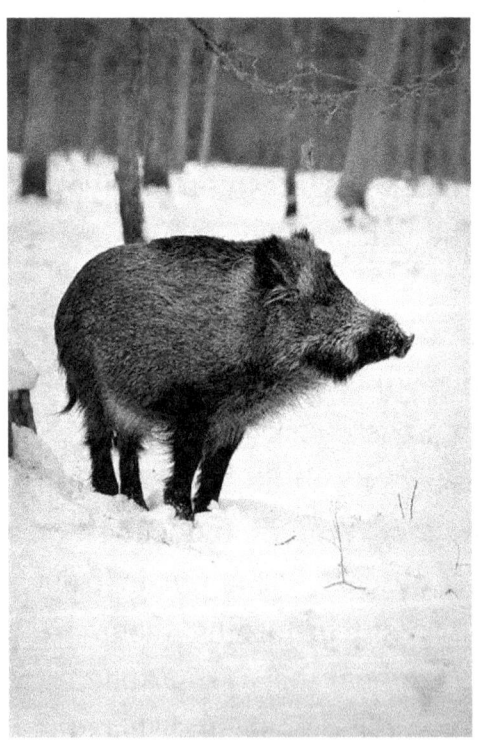

- Choose the best national parks and biosphere reserves to visit: If you want to have a guided and organised wildlife safari in Poland, you can choose from several national parks and biosphere reserves that offer wildlife tours and safaris. For example, you can visit the Babia Góra National Park, which offers guided hikes and bike rides to see the Tatra chamois, the brown bear, and the alpine flora. You can also visit the Białowieża National Park, which offers guided walks and horse-drawn carriage rides to see the bison, the wolf, and the lynx. You can also visit the Słowiński National Park, which offers guided boat trips and birdwatching tours to see the white-tailed eagle, the crane, and the mute swan. You can also visit the West Polesie Biosphere Reserve, which offers guided canoe trips and beaver watching tours to see the beaver, the otter, and the European pond turtle.

Conclusion

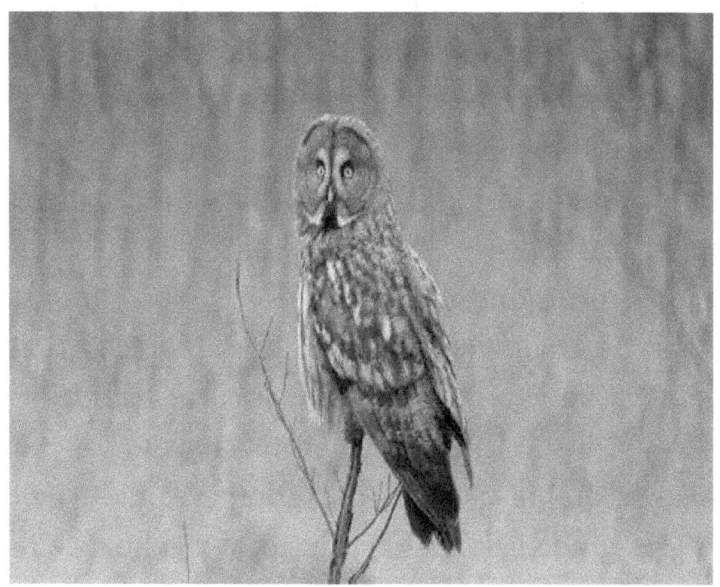

Polish wildlife is a precious and irreplaceable part of the natural and cultural heritage of Poland, as well as a source of beauty, wealth, and pride. However, it also faces many challenges and threats in the future, such as habitat loss, climate change, pollution, hunting, and invasive species. These factors can affect the survival and well-being of many animal species and ecosystems, and require urgent and effective solutions and actions. Fortunately, there are also many opportunities and solutions that can help conserve and enhance Polish wildlife, such as education, research, legislation, management, and restoration.

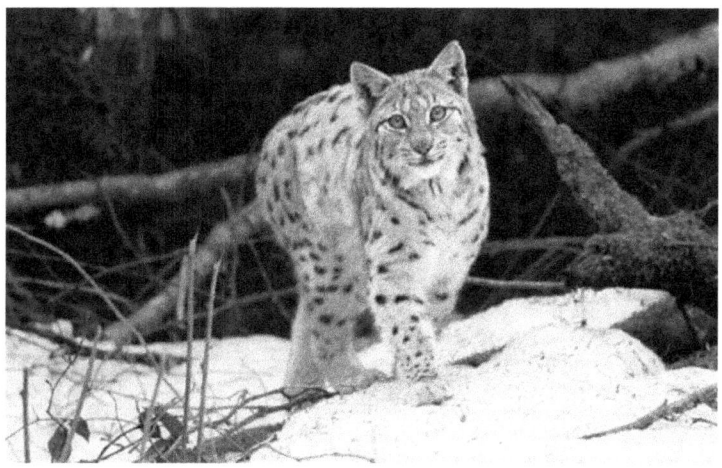

These actions can benefit both wildlife and humans, by improving the quality and quantity of the resources and services that they depend on, as well as the resilience and diversity of the environment. Therefore, we call on all stakeholders and actors involved in wildlife issues, such as government, non-government, private, and local organisations, as well as individuals and communities, to work together and cooperate for the future of Polish wildlife. We believe that with knowledge, awareness, and appreciation, we can achieve a peaceful and harmonious coexistence with wildlife, and ensure its protection and prosperity for generations to come.

If you enjoyed this piece, please leave a review to enable me to create more amazing content.

If you want more books similar to this, leave your suggestions in the review detailing which country's wildlife you would like me to write about next.

www.ingramcontent.com/pod-product-compliance
Lightning Source LLC
Chambersburg PA
CBHW072336290526
45794CB00002B/897